Counsell

Know Yourself

An explanation of the oneness of being

From Arabic manuscripts attributed to
Muhyiddin Ibn 'Arabi
and also to
Awhad al-din Balyani

Translation and introduction by
CECILIA TWINCH

Beshara Publications

Published by Beshara Publications
PO Box 33, Northleach
Cheltenham GL54 3WU, UK
www.besharapublications.org.uk

© English translation, Cecilia Twinch 2011

First published 2011
Reprinted 2014, 2017, 2018, 2021

British Library Cataloguing in Publication Data.
A catalogue record for this book is available from
the British Library.

ISBN: 978 0 904975 65 9

Cover design by Marijke van Basten Batenburg
Cover image © Hiroko Nagato-Apthorp, 2011

Printed and bound in the UK by
Windrush Group, Witney, Oxford

We are speaking with those who have determination and energy in seeking knowledge of their self in order to know God, and who keep fresh in their heart the image of their seeking and longing for union with God.

Contents

Acknowledgements

With special thanks to Bulent Rauf
who introduced me to this work in the
early seventies

Thanks also to Jane Carroll, Judy Kearns, Julia Dry,
Marijke van Basten Batenburg, Michael Tiernan,
Adam Dupré, Martin Notcutt, Jane Clark, Rosemary
Brass, Stephen Hirtenstein, Samaa Almahasni, Robert
MacLean, and Robert Clark.

Introduction

You yourself are the object of your quest

This short book introduces a view of the world which is very different to that held by many people. For some, it may serve a purpose in shattering preconceived notions and presenting an entirely new perspective which opens up a compassionate and responsive universe. It reflects an ardent desire to reach beyond the peripheral uncertainties of everyday life and discover, for ourselves, a certainty in the oneness of being which constantly flows through everything that is.

This is a new translation of the first complete work attributed to Ibn 'Arabi to appear in a western language. The earlier translation has been instrumental in making Ibn 'Arabi's name known again in the West over the last century, even though the author of the book is now considered by many scholars to be Balyani, a near contemporary, who may well have been influenced by his thought.

The translation has been made using several Arabic manuscripts from libraries in the UK, Turkey and Syria. The sheer quantity of manuscripts available shows how popular this book has remained for more than seven centuries and how many times it has been copied and recopied by hand. It should be borne in mind, however, that each time a manuscript is copied a few mistakes, alterations and added notes by the copyist may creep in. So although the text remains basically the same, there are often many minor variations on the general theme. In particular, there are also variations on the title and the author to whom the work is attributed.

The most popular title for the book is the *Treatise on Unity* (*Risalat al-ahadiyya*), which is similar to the title of a work which is definitely by Ibn 'Arabi, *The Book of Unity* (*Kitab al-ahadiyya*) or *The Book of Alif*.[1]

---

1. This may explain some of the confusion that has arisen over the authorship of the work. However, the content of these two books is quite different. See *Rasa'il Ibn 'Arabi* (Beirut: Dar Sadir, 1997), pp. 44–57; translated into English by Abraham Abadi in *Journal of the Muhyiddin Ibn 'Arabi Society*, 2 (1984), pp. 15–40.

Other titles include: *Treatise on Being, The Book of Alif, The Book of Answers, The Book of the Self or He (huwa), Treatise of Absolute Oneness, On the Secrets of Unity (tawhid), On the Oneness of Being and the Knower of God*. Many of the manuscripts have as the title or as a sub-title: *On the meaning of the saying of the Prophet Muhammad, peace on him, 'Whoever knows their self knows their Lord'*.

This edition of *Know Yourself* is intended to be as accessible as possible to people with no knowledge of Arabic and who do not necessarily have much knowledge of the cultural context of the book. In medieval Arabic, no capital letters or punctuation were used. Occasionally, in some manuscripts, the title and particular phrases – for example, *If someone asks you* and *Then the answer is* – are written in reddish brown ink to distinguish them from the black ink of the rest of the text. In modern printing we can use layout and italics to help make the text clear, as for example in the way the poems are set out, whereas in the Arabic text, it usually simply says 'Poem' to indicate where one begins. As well as for the phrases already mentioned above, in this

3

edition, italics have been used instead of quotation marks to indicate speech, quotations from the Quran and traditional sayings of the Prophet Muhammad. There is a list of these at the back of the book, with Quranic references where appropriate. To help the flow of the text, there are no notes in the text itself. There are some translator's notes after the text to explain key terms and concepts.

Ibn 'Arabi (d.1240)

The world is imagination,
Yet in reality it is Real.[2]

Ibn 'Arabi was born in Murcia, Spain in 1165 and spent half his life in the West and half in the East. When he was eight years old he moved with his family to Seville, where he was based for the remainder of his time in Spain, although he travelled a great deal both in Andalusia and North Africa. As a young teenager, he felt a strong calling from

2. *Fusus al-hikam*, ed. A. 'Affifi (Beirut: Dar al-Kitab al-Arabi, 1946), p. 159. See the poem at the end of the Chapter on Solomon in the English translations listed in the Bibliography.

God and went into retreat. During this time he had a spiritual vision, under the guidance of the three prophets of the Abrahamic religions, Jesus, Moses and Muhammad. He studied Islamic scriptures and all the traditional sciences, learning from many spiritual masters,[3] and he began to write books. Throughout his life, he continued to have innumerable mystical experiences, visions and realizations and had countless encounters with extraordinary individuals engaged on the spiritual way.

In 1200 he started his journey to the East, passing through North Africa, Egypt, Hebron (the burial place of Abraham) and the Dome of the Rock in Jerusalem, on his way to perform the pilgrimage in Mecca. He settled for a while in Anatolia where he educated Sadruddin al-Qunawi as his spiritual heir; Sadruddin al-Qunawi was a contemporary of Rumi and later, in Konya, the two became close friends and colleagues. Ibn 'Arabi continued to travel extensively in Anatolia, Iraq and the major cities of

---

3. See R.W.J. Austin, *Sufis of Andalusia* (Sherborne, Glos.: Beshara Publications, 1988).

the Middle East. All the time he was writing and giving spiritual advice to those who sought it. Finally he settled in Damascus, where he is buried.

Ibn 'Arabi wrote more than 300 books of which about 93 have survived to the present day. Many more works have been attributed to him, but recent research has shown that many of these were not in fact written by him. His principal works are the *Fusus al-hikam* (*The Ringstones of Wisdom*) and the *Futuhat al-makkiyya* (*Meccan Revelations*).[4] His work is becoming increasingly well known in the West as more translations, studies and articles about him become available.

He is most famous for his teachings on the oneness of being (*wahdat al-wujud*) and human perfection. Ibn 'Arabi describes the world as the exteriorization of a single hidden reality. All that we see as creation is a divine self-revelation which is constantly renewed in different forms at every moment. Of all

4. See Bibliography for English translations of the *Fusus* and passages from the *Futuhat*.

creation, human beings have the capacity to receive the complete revelation since they encompass all levels of existence. Every human being has the potential to become a complete mirror to Reality, therefore integrating all aspects of life in a balanced and appropriate way. Above all, the movement of existence is the movement of love for the sake of the revelation of beauty.

Ibn 'Arabi remains one of the most influential figures in the Islamic world. As S.H. Nasr has said: 'It would not be an exaggeration to say that Ibn 'Arabi is the most influential intellectual figure in the Islamic world during the past seven centuries, if the whole world is considered.'[5]

Today, his work is once again becoming increasingly well known in the West where he was born, due to the universal aspect of his thought. There is now a wealth of information about his life and work

5. Seyyed Hossein Nasr, *Islamic Philosophy from its Origin to the Present* (Albany, NY: SUNY Press, 2006), p. 135.

emerging from research and scholarship,[6] and many translations of his works into English and other European languages.

Awhad al-din Balyani (d.1287)

The Truth: you can't see any other than God,
For no doubt both worlds aren't other than Him![7]

Awhad al-din Balyani, also known as Abu 'Abdallah Balyani, was a Sufi Shaykh from the region of Persia known as Shiraz. Very little is known about him for certain and his name is currently only heard of within academic or Sufi circles. In their research on him, both Michel Chodkiewicz[8] and James W.

6. See, for example, Stephen Hirtenstein, *The Unlimited Mercifier: The spiritual life and thought of Ibn 'Arabi* (Oxford: Anqa Publishing, 1999).

7. From a poem by Balyani quoted in James W. Morris, 'Jami's description of Abu Abdallah Balyani: Theophany or "Pantheism"?: the Importance of Balyani's *Risalat al-Ahadiyya*', in *Horizons Maghrebins*, 30 (Toulouse, Winter 1995), pp. 43–50.

8. Michel Chodkiewicz, *Épître sur l'Unicité Absolue* (*Treatise on Absolute Unity – Risalat al-wahda al-mutlaqa*), (Paris: Les Deux Océans, 1982).

Morris[9] have relied heavily on the biographical note in a 15th-century book on the lives of the saints, *Nafahat al-uns* (*The Breaths of Intimacy*), by the Persian writer Jami (d.1492),[10] who was from the school of Ibn 'Arabi and wrote a famous commentary on Ibn 'Arabi's *Fusus al-hikam* (*The Ringstones of Wisdom*).

We learn from Jami that Balyani was descended from a line of Sufis going back to Abu 'Ali Daqqaq whose son-in-law and spiritual heir was Qushayri (d.1074), author of the important *Epistle on Sufism* which Ibn 'Arabi mentions in his book about the Sufis of Andalusia.[11] Spiritually, he was descended from Abu Najib al-Suhrawardi (d.1168), founder of the Suhrawardiyya Sufi order. From this we can see that Balyani was steeped in Sufi culture. In addition, we are told that he lived in seclusion on

9. See note 7 above.

10. 'Abd al-Rahman Jami, *Nafahat al-uns*, ed. M. Tawhidipur (Tehran: 1957), pp. 258–62.

11. See Austin, *Sufis of Andalusia*, p. 71. Abu'l-Qasim al-Qushayri, *Al-Qushayri's Epistle on Sufism*, trans. Alexander Knysh (Reading: Garnet, 2007).

Mount Ligam for eleven years and spent time with Sufi masters. Balyani reported that his father used to say, 'Whatever I requested from God, I gave to (my son) 'Abdallah; what God opened up to me like a little peephole, He opened up for (my son) like a wide-open gate.'[12]

Elsewhere, Balyani has been described as a disciple of the mystical poet Shushtari (d.1269). Shushtari was an outstanding student of the Andalusian Ibn Sab'in (d.1270), a close contemporary of Ibn 'Arabi. Ibn Sab'in was also born in Murcia, like Ibn 'Arabi, and spent time in North Africa, Egypt and Mecca, where he died. Despite the many differences between the understanding of what became known as the oneness of being or unity of existence (*wahdat al-wujud*) in Ibn 'Arabi and Ibn Sab'in, it is quite likely that Ibn 'Arabi's work and thought made a definite impression on Ibn Sab'in. One possible difference is that both Ibn Sab'in and Balyani tend to emphasize the illusory nature of the world. Ibn

12. Morris, 'Jami's description', p. 47; see also Chodkiewicz, *Épître*, p. 22.

'Arabi, on the other hand, does not deny the reality of the world but rather he sees the world as the place of God's self-revelation.

Balyani's insistence on 'Only God' has led some commentators to see this book as potentially dangerous in its ability to cause misunderstandings about the nature of reality when taken without the support of its entire spiritual and cultural context, and the practical training which that entails. This may well have been true in past times, but in today's global society, where information about anything and everything is generally so readily available, each individual needs to discriminate and discern the value of what is offered, for themselves. At the same time, it does not remove the need to find reliable, practical guidance on the spiritual path, to use one's common sense, to apply rational consideration and intellectual rigour, and to observe appropriate moral obligations and responsibilities. This book is a brief, poetic glimpse emerging from a whole spiritual and cultural framework. Although it can be read as a self-standing work, the cautionary tale that follows should also be taken into account.

In the introduction to his translation of Balyani's *Epistle on Absolute Unicity*,[13] Michel Chodkiewicz recounts this story about Shaykh Awhad al-din Balyani, which was set down by Jami in his book *Nafahat al-uns* (*Breaths of Intimacy*):[14]

One of the students of the Shaykh was in retreat on a mountain. A snake came near him and he tried to grab hold of it. The snake bit him and his limbs began to swell. The Shaykh came to know about this and sent for his student.

He then said to him, 'Why did you grab hold of the snake, so that it bit you?'

'Oh master,' replied the student, 'you yourself said that there is nothing but God. On seeing the snake, I saw only God. Plucking up courage, I grabbed hold of it!'

13. Chodkiewicz, *Épître*, pp. 22–3.

14. My translation of the story is from Chodkiewicz's French version, *Épître*, pp. 22–3; also translated by Morris in his article 'Jami's description', p. 48.

The Shaykh replied, 'When God manifests himself to you under the aspect of terrifying power, run away! Don't approach Him, otherwise the same thing will happen to you again!'

Then he sat him down and said to him, 'Hold back from acting so boldly until you know Him perfectly.'

After that he recited some invocations and blew on him. The swelling went down and the student was healed.

Know Yourself

An explanation of the oneness of being

On the meaning of the saying of the
Prophet Muhammad
(God bless him and give him peace)

Whoever knows their self, knows their Lord

In the name of God,
the compassionate, the merciful

Praise belongs to God, before whose oneness
there is no before unless the before is He
and after whose singleness there is no after
unless the after is He. He is, and there is not
with Him any before or after, above or below,
closeness or distance, how or where or when,
time or moment or duration, manifested
existence or place. *And He is now as He has
always been.* He is the one without oneness
and the single without singleness. He is not
composed of name and named, for His name
is Him and His named is Him and there is no

17

name or named other than Him. He is the first without firstness and the last without lastness. He is the apparent without appearance and the hidden without hiddenness.
I mean that He is the very existence of the letters of the names the first and the last, the apparent and the hidden. There is no first or last, apparent or hidden except Him, without the letters which form these divine names becoming Him and without Him becoming these letters.

Understand this so as not to make the mistake of those who believe in incarnation. He is not in anything and no thing is in Him, whether entering into Him or coming out of Him. It is in this way that you should know Him and not through theoretical knowledge, reason, understanding or conjecture, nor with the senses, the external

eye or interior sight or perception. No one
sees Him except Himself, no one reaches
Him except Himself and no one knows Him
except Himself. He knows Himself through
Himself and He sees Himself by means of
Himself. No one but He sees Him. His veil
is His oneness since nothing veils Him other
than Him. His own being veils Him. His
being is concealed by His oneness without
any condition.

No one other than He sees Him. No sent
prophet, perfect saint or angel brought close
knows Him. His prophet is He, His messen-
ger is He, His message is He and His word is
He. He sent Himself from Himself, through
Himself to Himself. There is no intermediary or means other than Him. There is no
difference between the sender, that which is
sent and the one to whom it is sent. The very

existence of the prophetic message is His existence. There is no existence to any other who could pass away, or have a name or be named.

Because of this, the Prophet, God bless him and give him peace, said, *Whoever knows their self, knows their Lord*. He also said, *I knew my Lord through my Lord*. What the Prophet pointed out by that, is that you are not you but you are Him and there is no you. It is not that He enters into you or that you enter into Him, or that He comes out of you or that you come out of Him. That does not mean that you have being and you are qualified by this or that attribute. What is meant is that you never were and never will be, whether through yourself or through Him or in Him or with Him. You have neither ceased to be nor are you existent. You are Him and He is you, without any of these imperfections. If you know your existence in this way, then you know God, and if not, then not.

Most of those who claim to know God make the knowledge of God dependent on the passing away of existence and on the passing away of that passing away. That is clearly an error and misconception. The knowledge of God does not require the passing away of existence or the passing away of that passing away because things have no existence and what does not exist cannot pass away. Passing away implies the prior existence of the thing that passes away. If you know yourself without existing and passing away, then you know God, and if not, then not.

By making the knowledge of God dependent on the passing away of your existence and the passing away of that passing away, there is an affirmation of something other than God. The Prophet said, *Whoever knows their self, knows their Lord.* He did not say, *Whoever annihilates their self, knows their Lord.*

Your being is nothing and whatever is nothing cannot be placed in relationship to anything else, whether it is capable of passing away or not and whether it is existent or nonexistent. The Prophet alluded to the fact that you are nonexistent now as you were nonexistent before creation, because now is eternity-without-beginning and now is eternity-without-end and now is timelessness. God is the very being of eternity-without-beginning, eternity-without-end and timelessness even though in reality there is no eternity-without-beginning, eternity-without-end or timelessness. If it were otherwise,

He would not be alone, without any associate. However, it is necessary for Him to be alone without any associate because any associate would exist through itself, and not through the being of God. Then that associate would not need God and would therefore be a second Lord, which is impossible. God has no associate, equal or like.

Whoever sees anything with God, whether coming out of Him or within Him, but dependent on Him by virtue of His lordship, has also made that thing an associate even though that associate depends on Him by virtue of His lordship. Whoever allows that there could be anything with God – whether subsisting by itself or through Him, whether in a state of having passed away or the passing away of passing away – is far from breathing the scent of self-knowledge.

Because whoever accepts that there could be any being other than Him, yet subsisting through Him and in Him, then passing away in successive stages of passing away and passing away of passing away – which is polytheism upon polytheism and not knowledge of the self at all – is a polytheist [who believes in many gods] and does not know God or themselves.

If someone asks: What is the way to knowledge of the self and knowledge of God?

The answer is: It consists in being aware that *God is, and nothing is with Him. And He is now as He has always been.*

If someone then says: I see myself as other than God and I do not see God as myself.

The answer is: The Prophet meant by the word 'self' your being and your essential reality, and not the self which is called the blaming self or the lower self or the self which is known as the confident and peaceful self. By the self, he was alluding to everything that is other than God, like when he said, O God, *show me things as they are*, indicating by 'things' whatever is other than God; that is, *Make me know what is other than You, so that I may know what things really are – whether they are You or other than You, whether they are eternal and subsistent, or newly happening and temporal.*

Then God showed him what is other than Him as Himself, without the existence of what is other than Him. So he saw things as they are, that is, he saw them as the essence of God, who is exalted, without how or

where. The word 'things' applies to the self
and to other things, because the existence of
the self and the existence of things are equal
in terms of being 'things'. When you know
the things, you know yourself and when you
know yourself, you know the Lord. Because
what you think is other than God is not
other than God but you do not know it.
You see Him and you do not know that you
see Him.

When this secret is revealed to you, you will
know that you are not other than God but
that you yourself are the object of your quest.
You do not need to get rid of your self. You
have not ceased, nor will you cease, to exist,
without time and without moments, as we
have already mentioned. You will see His
attributes as your attributes, your exterior
as His exterior, your interior as His interior,

your first as His first and your last as His last, without any doubt or uncertainty. You will see your attributes to be His attributes and your essence to be His essence, without you becoming Him and without Him becoming you in the least degree.

Everything passes away except His face, both outwardly and inwardly. This means that there is no existent but Him. Nothing other than Him has being and therefore has to pass away so that His face remains. There is nothing except His face.

It is as if a person who does not know something, then comes to know it. Their existence does not disappear, but their ignorance disappears. Their existence remains as it was, without being exchanged for another, and without the existence of the ignorant person being added to, or mixed with, the knowing person: ignorance simply disappears.

Do not think therefore that you need to pass away, because if it were necessary to pass away, that would mean that you are His veil. He would therefore be veiled by something other than Himself. This would require something other than Him having power over Him, which prevents Him from being seen. That is an error and misconception. As we have already said, His veil is nothing other than His oneness and His singularity. That is why the person who has reached the essential truth is allowed to say, *I am the truth* or *Glory to me*. No one has truly reached Him, unless they see their attributes to be the attributes of God and their essence to be the essence of God, without their essence or their attributes ever entering into God or coming out of Him and without passing away in relation to God or remaining in God. They see that their self has never been their own, not that it was and then it passed away. Because there is no self except His self, and there is no being except His being. This is what the Prophet was alluding to when he said, *Do not curse time, because God is time*, and God, who is blessed and exalted, is unblemished by any associate or equal or like.

It is also reported that the Prophet said *The high God says, 'O child of Adam, I was sick and you did not visit Me, I was hungry and you did not feed Me, I asked of you and you did not give to Me...'*. This alludes to the fact that the being of the person who asks is His being. When that is accepted, it is also accepted that your being is His being, and the being of all created things, whether substance or accident, is His being.

When the secret of an atom is discovered, the secret of all created things is made clear, whether they are apparent or hidden. You do not see the two worlds as other than God, without the two worlds and their names and what they name existing – or rather, their names and what they name and their existence are Him, without any doubt. You do not see God as having ever created anything but as being *every day in a different configuration* which sometimes reveals Him and sometimes conceals Him, without any condition, since *He is the first and the last, the apparent and the hidden and He has knowledge of everything*. He manifests Himself in His oneness and hides Himself in His singularity. He is the first in His essence and His self-

subsistence and the last in His everlasting-
ness. He is the very being of the name the
first and the name the last, of the name the
apparent and the name the hidden. He is His
own name and what is named. Just as His
existence is necessary, the nonexistence of
what is other than Him is necessary. What
you think is other than Him is not other
than Him. He is free from there being any
other than Him. Indeed, other than Him is
Him without any otherness, whether this is
with Him or in Him, inwardly or outwardly.

Whoever is qualified in this way has innumerable attributes, without limit or end.
Just as the person whose physical form
passes away is deprived of all their attributes
whether praiseworthy or blameworthy, so
the person who dies a mystical death has
all their attributes, whether praiseworthy

or blameworthy, taken away from them and God comes into their place in all their states. The essence of God comes into the place of their essence and the attributes of God come into the place of their attributes. Because of this, the Prophet said, *Die before you die*, that is, *Know yourself before you die*. He also said, *God says, 'My servant continues to approach Me with free acts until I love him. And when I love him, I am his hearing, his sight, his hand...'*, which refers to the fact that whoever knows their self sees their whole being as the very being of God, without any change in their essence or attributes. There is no need for any change since that person was not the existence of their own essence but was simply ignorant of the knowledge of their self.

When you know yourself, your egoism disappears and you know that you are no other than God. If you had an independent existence, you would have no need of passing away or of self-knowledge. You would therefore be a lord apart from Him, but there is no lord apart from God, who is blessed and exalted.

The benefit of the knowledge of the self is to know for certain that you are neither existent nor nonexistent, that you are not, never have been and never will be. In this way, the meaning of *There is no god but God* becomes clear: there is no divinity other than Him, being belongs to none but Him, there is no other except Him, there is no god but He.

If someone says: You make His lordship superfluous.

The reply is: I do not make His lordship superfluous, because He has not stopped being both ruler and ruled, just as He has never stopped being both creator and what is created, *and He is now as He has always been*. His creativity and His lordship do not need what is created or subject to Him. When He brought the creatures into existence, He was already endowed with all His attributes, *and He is now as He has always been*. There is no difference in His oneness between the new and the eternal: the new requires His manifestation and the eternal requires His remaining hidden. His exterior is identical to His interior and His interior is identical to His exterior; His first is the same as His last and His last is the same as His first and all is one and the one is all. He was described as *every day in a different configuration* when there was no 'thing' other than Him. *And He is now as He has always been*,

since in reality what is other than Him has no
being. Just as in eternity-without-beginning
and timelessness, He was *every day in a different configuration* when no thing existed, so *He
is now as He has always been,* although there is
no thing or day, just as there has been from all
eternity no thing or day. The existence of the
creatures and their nonexistence are the same.
If it were not so, it would require the origina-
tion of something which was not already in
His oneness. That would imply imperfection
and His oneness is far more exalted than that.

When you know yourself in this way, without
attributing any opposite, like, equal or associate to God, then you really know yourself.
That is why the Prophet said, *Whoever knows
their self, knows their Lord* and not *Whoever
gets rid of their self, knows their Lord* because
he knew and saw that there is nothing other

than Him. Then he pointed out that the knowledge of the self is the knowledge of God. In other words, *Know yourself* or *Know your being*, because you are not you but you do not know it. That is, know that your being is neither your being nor other than your being. You are neither existent nor nonexistent, nor other than existent nor other than nonexistent. Your being and your non-being are His being, without any being or absence of being because your being and your non-being are the same as His being and His being is the same as your being and non-being.

So if you see things without seeing anything else with God or in God, but see things as Him, then you know yourself and such a knowledge of the self is knowledge of God, without doubt or uncertainty and without mixing anything temporal with the eternal, whether in Him or through Him.

If someone now asks you: What is the way to union when you assert that there is no other than Him, yet one thing cannot be united to itself?

Then this is the reply: There is no doubt that in reality there is neither union nor separation, distance or closeness, since union is only possible between two things and if there is only one there can be neither union nor separation. Union requires two things which are either similar – in which case they are equal, or dissimilar – in which case they are opposites. However, He is exalted far above having any opposite or equal. Therefore union lies in something other than union, closeness in something other than closeness and distance in something other than distance. There is union without union, closeness without closeness and distance without distance.

If someone asks: We understand union without union, but what does closeness without closeness and distance without distance mean?

Then the answer is: I mean that in those times of closeness and distance you were not anything other than God, but you did not know yourself and you were not aware that you were always Him, without 'you'. When you reach God, that is, when you know yourself in a way that is beyond all condition, you know that you are Him, and you did not know before whether you were Him or other than Him. When knowledge comes upon you, you know that it is through God that you know God, not through yourself.

Suppose, for example, that you do not know that your name is Mahmud, or that what your name designates (your named) is Mahmud – for the name and the named are in fact one and the same thing – and that you think that your name is Muhammad. If you then learn that you are really Mahmud, you do not stop being who you were. The name Muhammad is simply taken away from you because of your knowledge of yourself – that you are Mahmud and you were only Muhammad by ceasing to be yourself. Because ceasing to be presupposes the affirmation of the existence of what is other than Him, and then whoever affirms the existence of what is other than Him has attributed an associate to Him. Nothing has been taken away from Mahmud: Muhammad did not pass away into Mahmud and Mahmud did not enter into Muhammad or come out of him, nor did Mahmud become incarnated in Muhammad. When Mahmud knew himself, that he was Mahmud and not Muhammad, he knew himself through himself and not through Muhammad. Because Muhammad never was, so how could anything be known through him?

Therefore the knower and the known, the one who arrives and what he arrives at, and the seer and the seen are one. 'The knower' is His attribute and 'the known' is His essence, and 'the one who arrives' is His attribute and 'what he arrives at' is His essence. In fact, the attribute and that to which it is attributed are one. That is the explanation of the saying, *Whoever knows their self, knows their Lord.*

Whoever understands this example knows that there is no union or separation. The knower is He and the known is He, the one who sees is He and what is seen is He, the one who arrives is He and what he arrives at is He. No other than He reaches union, no other than He separates from Him. Whoever understands this is free of the polytheism of polytheism, and whoever has not understood this has not breathed the scent of this freedom from polytheism.

Most of 'those who know', who think that they know themselves and their Lord and think that they are free of the bonds of existence, declare that the way can only be travelled by passing away, then by the passing away of passing away. That is because they do not understand the saying of the Prophet and, believing themselves to be free of polytheism, they allude sometimes to the negation of existence, that is, to the passing away of existence, sometimes to the passing away of passing away, and sometimes to extinction or annihilation. All these expressions are unadulterated polytheism because whoever accepts that there could be anything other than Him which is subsequently capable of passing away, then of passing away from passing away, affirms that there is something other than Him, and whoever affirms that is a polytheist. May God guide them and us to the right path.

> You thought you were you,
> But you are not you and never were.
> For if you were you, you would be a lord
> And the second of two. Stop what
>   you were thinking.

Between His being and your being
    there is no difference.
He is no different from you nor
    you from Him.
If you say in ignorance you are other,
    you are stubborn,
But if your ignorance disappears,
    you are submissive.
For your union is separation,
    your separation union,
And your distance is closeness –
    through that you become suitable.
Abandon the intellect and understand
    by the light of unveiling,
So that what you are safeguarding
    does not escape you.
Do not debase yourself by associating
    other with God,
For associating other with
    God is debasing.

If someone says: You point out that your knowledge of yourself is the knowledge of God, but the one who knows their self is other than God. So how can that which is other than God know God and reach union with Him?

The answer is: Whoever knows their self knows that their being is not their being, nor other than their being, but that they are the very being of God, without their being becoming the being of God or entering into God or coming out of Him, and without their being existing along with Him or in Him. They see their being as it was before coming into being, without the need for passing away, effacement or the passing away of passing away. For the passing away of something implies that it was previously existent and that in turn implies that it exists

44

by itself and not by the power of God, which is clearly impossible. It is evident that the knowledge that the knower has of their self is the knowledge that God has of Himself, because their self is no other than He.

By the word 'self', the Prophet meant 'being'. The being of the one who reaches this spiritual level is no longer their being whether inwardly or outwardly, but it is the very being of God. Their speech is His speech, their actions are God's actions and their claim to the knowledge of God is their claim to the knowledge God has of Himself through Himself. But you hear this claim as though coming from that person, you see their actions as though coming from them, you see them to be other than God, just as you see yourself as other than God because of your ignorance of your real being. For *the faithful one is the mirror of the Faithful One*, so he is He in His eye, that is, through His sight. For if his eye is God's eye and his sight is God's sight, without any condition, he is not He through your eye or your knowledge, understanding, imagination, thought or vision, but he is He in His eye, His knowledge and His vision. Then if he says *I am God*, listen to him, because it is God who is saying *I am God*, not him. But you have not reached the point that he has reached, since if you had arrived at it, you would understand what he says, you would say what he says and you would see what he sees.

To summarize, the existence of things is His existence, without them existing. But do not fall into confusion and do not let these allusions lead you to imagine that God is created. One of those who know has said,

The Sufi is uncreated. It is like that after the complete unveiling and dissipation of doubts and conjecturing. But this spiritual nourishment is only for the person whose nature is larger than the two worlds. As for the person whose nature is only as large as the two worlds, it is not suitable for them, for it is greater than the two worlds.

Finally, you need to know that the seer and the seen, the one who finds and what is found, the knower and the known, the creator and the created, the perceiver and the perceived are one. He sees, knows and perceives His being by means of His being, beyond any manner of sight, knowledge and perception and without the existence of the form of sight, knowledge and perception. Just as His being is beyond all condition, so the vision, knowledge and perception which He has of Himself are without condition.

If someone asks: How do you view all the repulsive and desirable things? For example, when we see dung or carrion, do we say it is God?

Then the reply is: God forbid that God, who is exalted and sanctified, should be any such thing. Our conversation is with those who do not see dung as dung, or carrion as carrion. We are only speaking with those who are endowed with inner vision and not with those who are inwardly blind. Anyone who does not know their self is blind and does not see. Until their blindness and lack of vision disappears, they will not grasp these meanings. Our conversation is with God, not with other than God and not with the inwardly blind. Whoever reaches this spiritual station knows that they are no other than God. We are speaking with those who have determination and energy in seeking knowledge of their self in order to know God, and who keep fresh in their heart the image of their seeking and longing for union with God, and not with those without aim or intention.

If someone objects: God has declared that *Eyes do not perceive Him but He perceives the eyes, He is the subtle and well-informed one*, yet you maintain the contrary, so what you are saying is not true.

Then the response is: Everything that we are saying is the very meaning of God's words, *Eyes do not perceive Him, but He perceives the eyes*, that is, there is no one else in existence, so no one has sight which can perceive Him.

49

If it were conceivable that there were someone other than Him, then it would follow that this other could perceive Him. But God has informed us in His saying *Eyes do not perceive Him* that there is no other except Him. This means that no other than He perceives Him, that is, He who perceives Him is Himself. There is no other than He. He is the one who perceives His essence, not another. Eyes do not perceive Him because they are nothing but His being. Whoever maintains that eyes do not perceive Him because they are transient and what is transient cannot grasp what is eternal and everlasting, still does not know their self. For there is nothing, and there are no eyes which are not Him. He perceives His own being without the existence of perception, without condition and without other.

I knew the Lord through the Lord
  without doubt or uncertainty.
My essence is really His essence
  without lack or imperfection.
There is no otherness between them
  and my self is the place where
    the invisible appears.
Since I have known myself
  without mixture or blemish,
I have reached union with my beloved
  without distance or closeness.
I received a gift overflowing
  without any giving or intermingling.
My self did not vanish in Him
  nor does the one who vanished remain.

If someone asks: You affirm God and you deny
the existence of everything else, so what are
these things that you see?

The answer is this: These words are for those who see nothing other than God. We have no discussion with those who do see something other than God, for they only see what they see. Whoever knows their self sees nothing except God, but whoever does not know their self, does not see God. Each receptacle only exudes what is in it. We have already explained a great deal and if we explained more, whoever does not see will still not see, understand or comprehend; but whoever does see, sees, understands and comprehends already. A hint is enough for the one who has reached union. As for the person who has not reached union, they will not arrive by theoretical teaching, instruction, repetition, reason or learning, but only by putting themselves in the service of an eminent master who has arrived and a wise teacher, following the spiritual path in order

to be guided by their light and progress by
means of their spiritual will, and reaching in
this way what they are seeking, if God wills.

May God grant us success in what He loves
and in what satisfies Him in word and deed,
knowledge and practice, light and guidance.
He has power over everything and is able to
respond to every request. There is no power
or ability except in God, the sublime, the
magnificent.

Peace and blessings on the Prophet,
his family and friends.

Translator's notes on the text

The self or soul (*nafs*)

*The Prophet meant by the word 'self' your being and
your essential reality, and not the self which is called the
blaming self or the lower self or the self which is known
as the confident and peaceful self.*

The Arabic word for self (*nafs*) has many different meanings. It can be used reflexively[1] or it can
mean soul. Occasionally, it is used in the same way
as 'spirit' (*ruh*) but more often it is considered as
an intermediary between the spirit and the body.
Sometimes it is used in the sense of the qualities of
the human person, but it is frequently used as an
equivalent to what we now call the ego. However, in
the Quran it is also used of God, for example when
Jesus says to God, *You know what is in my self but I do
not know what is in Your self.*[2]

1. An example of a reflexive verb: 'She washed herself'
rather than 'She washed her face', or her child or anything else.
2. Quran, sura 5, verse 116 (Q.5:116), (verse 119 in some
editions).

The Quran also refers to three levels, or stages of development, of the self or soul. While the spirit within is always in a state of perfection, the soul may become tarnished. For many Sufis the perfecting of the self is a path of transformation which requires determination and effort, even though it is acknowledged that it can only be achieved through divine grace. The lowest level of the self mentioned in the Quran is 'the self which incites to evil',[3] often called the ego, the carnal self or the commanding self. Then when the person starts questioning their purpose in life and sets out on the spiritual way to knowledge of the self and of God, they become aware of their own shortcomings, weaknesses and lack of commitment and blame themselves for their deficiencies, which is the level of 'the blaming self'.[4] Finally, the self which is at the level of perfection is called 'the tranquil self or the soul at peace'.[5]

3. *Al-nafs al-ammara (bi-l-su')*, Q.12:53.
4. *Al-nafs al-lawwama*, Q.75:2.
5. *Al-nafs al-mutma'inna*, Q.89:27.

Notes on gender – He

This particular translation is intended to make the content of this book as accessible as possible to modern readers. In contemporary English, even official documents now use gender-neutral language. For example, 'they' is used as the singular pronoun instead of the masculine singular 'he', which nowadays is perceived to be gender-specific to males only. The use of the male 'he' in English translations sometimes creates an obstacle to understanding the meaning of the text for those who do not know Arabic. For this reason, when a single human person is being referred to in this text, the plural 'they' is used in accordance with current English usage. This includes the words of the Prophet, *Whoever knows their self knows their Lord* (*man ʿarafa nafsahu (faqad) ʿarafa rabbahu*) where the initial Arabic word '*man*' means 'whoever', 'everyone who', 'anybody who' and is not in itself gender-specific.[6] In the rest of

6. This is not the first time this saying has been translated as it is here. See James Winston Morris, 'Seeing Past the Shadows: Ibn ʿArabi's "Divine Comedy"', in *Journal of the Muhyiddin Ibn ʿArabi Society*, 12 (1992), pp. 58–9, where it is translated as:

the Arabic sentence, the masculine gender is used because in Arabic grammar, the masculine predominates over the feminine so where there is mixed gender, the masculine verb form is used. The Arabic word for Lord (*rabb*), which can also be translated as 'cherisher', 'sustainer', 'educator', is masculine, while the Arabic word for self or soul (*nafs*) is feminine so there are subtleties within this saying which do not appear in an English translation.

When it is God that is being referred to, as an ontologically active aspect of the one Reality, 'He' continues to be used. Of course, the ultimate ineffable Reality is without gender. However, in Arabic, while the primordial Essence is grammatically feminine, the active principle is masculine. This is the dynamic movement from the state of the absolute unknown, hidden Reality towards manifestation. The passage from the inexpressible to what is expressed allows for the possibility of relationship, as in the prophetic saying which Ibn 'Arabi is so fond of quoting, *I was a hidden treasure and I loved to be*

Whoever knows their soul/self, knows their Lord.

58

known, so I created the world… . In relationship to that moving, active principle the human being is receptive and in submission, like the part is to the whole.

The Arabic word for 'He' is *huwa.* It should be noted that in Arabic there is no neutral gender which is the equivalent of 'it' in English. When someone is present with us we refer to that person as you, but 'he' (the third person singular) is used when the person referred to is absent. The word for 'He-ness' or 'it-ness' (*huwiyya*)[7] refers to the essential self or the divine identity.

In his essay *Quantum, Chaos, and the Oneness of Being: Meditations on the Kitab al-Alef,*[8] Peter Lamborn Wilson remarks about the opening passage of Weir's translation of the present work:

7. See William C. Chittick, *Sufi Path of Knowledge* (Albany, NY: SUNY Press, 1989), p. 394, n. 15.

8. See Peter Lamborn Wilson, 'Quantum, Chaos, and the Oneness of Being: Meditations on the *Kitab al-Alef*', in *Muhyiddin Ibn 'Arabi: A Commemorative Volume*, ed. S. Hirtenstein and M. Tiernan (Shaftesbury, Dorset: Element, 1993), p. 366.

If the words 'God' and 'He' were replaced in this passage by the words 'reality' and 'it' and the words 'prophetic message' replaced with the words 'quantum theorems' or something like that, one might be excused for mistaking these lines for a discussion of quantum mechanics.

Passing away (*fana'*) and remaining (*baqa'*)

Most of 'those who know', who think that they know themselves and their Lord and think that they are free of the bonds of existence, declare that the way can only be travelled by passing away, then by the passing away of passing away.

As it has now become clear, this short book deals with the importance of self-knowledge. In particular, it emphasizes that, due to the unity of existence, there cannot be more than one being, and that is what is called God. In Islamic thought, the unity of God is often discussed in terms of the oneness of actions, the oneness of attributes and the oneness of Essence. Among Sufis, one of the major topics of discussion has been the idea of the passing away of the individual's existence and the passing away of the very idea of passing away, so that only the Real remains.

Many possible stages of passing away have been discussed. Sufis often refer to successive levels of realization where it is seen that ultimately the only actor is God, all names and attributes belong to God and even a person's individual essence is not their essence but an individuation of the One Essence. These stages are referred to as: the passing away of actions, the passing away of attributes and the passing away of the separate self in the Essence itself.

The Arabic terms for passing away (*fana'*) and remaining (*baqa'*) are based on the Quranic passage *Everything on earth passes away, but the face of your Lord, both majestic and magnanimous, remains.*[9] A similar idea is expressed in another verse quoted in this book: *Everything passes away (or perishes) except His face.*[10] The face reveals a person's identity and it refers to the essence or reality.

9. Q.55:26–7.
10. Q.28:88.

Ibn 'Arabi mentions the saying of one of the early Sufi masters: passing away is *the annihilation of he who was not* whereas remaining is *the subsistence of Him who has always been.*[11]

Fana' may also be translated as annihilation, ceasing to exist, non-being, vanishing, perishing, obliteration of the self, self-effacement, extinction (of individual consciousness), absorption (in God). 'Passing away' is usually 'from something' or 'in something', for example, passing away from one's self or being effaced in God. However, in this book it is often referred to as the passing away of existence (*fana' al-wujud*).

11. *Futuhat*, vol. III, p. 395; see William C. Chittick, *The Self-Disclosure of God* (Albany, NY: SUNY Press, 1998), p. 84.

Divine Names

*He is the first and the last, the apparent and the hidden
and He has knowledge of everything.*[12]

This often quoted Quranic verse is referred to from
the beginning of the book and may require some
explanation for those who are unfamiliar with its
context in Islam. In this verse, God calls Himself by
the names 'the first' and 'the last'. 'The first' refers
to the origin, the beginning and that which comes
before, while 'the last' refers to that which comes
after, until ending at the furthest limit when everything is returned to its origin. This happens at a particular time but it is also happening constantly at
every instant.

God also calls Himself by the names 'the apparent'
and 'the hidden', which are sometimes translated
as: the exterior and the interior, the outer and the
inner, the outward and the inward or the manifest
and the non-manifest.

12. Q.57:3.

63

Ibn 'Arabi explains that, at every moment, the hidden essence appears in a different form according to its place of appearance. It is apparent in all that we see while at the same time remaining hidden and invisible. Since there is nothing in existence but God, He is seen everywhere, according to the Quranic verse, *Wherever you turn, there is the face of God.*[13] Yet at the same time, God remains beyond our perception, *Eyes do not perceive Him:*[14] He is both transcendent and immanent, and He unites all opposites in Himself.

The divine names are attributed to God but we know them through the manifestation of their qualities in the world. In one sense they are the same as what they name because they simply describe different aspects of the same object named. However, in another sense they are different because each name has its own characteristics, and attributes a

13. Q.2:115. This is quoted in a few manuscripts of the text after the Quranic verse, *Everything passes away except His face*. However, only one of the manuscripts used in this translation contains this verse.

14. Q.6:103. Quoted in the text.

particular quality to the object named which is distinct from every other quality. Ibn 'Arabi says,

> The oneness (*ahadiyya*) of God with regard to the divine names, which require us, is the oneness of the many, and the oneness of God with regard to His being beyond need of us and His divine names, is the oneness of essence (*ahadiyyat al-'ayn*). The name the One (*al-ahad*) applies to both.[15]

The Letters

There is no first or last, apparent or hidden except Him, without the letters which form these divine names becoming Him or His becoming these letters.

In Islamic cosmology, the science of the letters has an important role. Both Ibn 'Arabi and Ibn Sab'in, who is thought to have had an influence on Balyani, had a knowledge of the science of the letters. Each

15. *Fusus al-hikam*, ed. 'Affifi, p. 105. See end of the Chapter on Joseph in the translations listed in the Bibliography: Austin, p. 126; Dagli, p. 103; Burckhardt/Culme-Seymour, p. 66; Bursevi/Rauf, p. 557.

name is composed of a particular combination of letters. It is through His word 'Be!'[16] that God brings all things into manifestation. This speech takes place through the breath of compassion in which all things become manifest.

Human speech also takes place through the breath. The first letter of the Arabic alphabet, which has the numerical value of one, is *alif*.[17] The *alif* by itself is silent.[18] It is the unimpeded breath represented graphically by a straight, vertical line. It is only pronounced if the first articulation is added to it (the *hamza*) although this letter may be considered as a pause or hiatus between silence and speech.[19] Then the first letter that is pronounced is the *ha* which is phonetically the most interior, coming with the

16. Q.16:40.

17. As this book is concerned with oneness, one of the titles that has been given to it is *The Book of Alif* which is also the title given to Ibn 'Arabi's *The Book of Alif* or *The Book of Unity*.

18. Ibn 'Arabi, *Contemplation of the Holy Mysteries*, trans. Cecilia Twinch and Pablo Beneito (Oxford: Anqa Publishing, 2001), p. 56.

19. See Titus Burckhardt, *Mystical Astrology According to Ibn 'Arabi* (Aldsworth, Glos.: Beshara Publications, 1977), pp. 32–5.

breath from the chest until a sound is produced in the throat. The last letter to be articulated is the *waw*, phonetically the most exterior being pronounced on the lips. These two letters make up the word *huwa* which unites all the letters from the first to the last, the most interior to the most exterior. In this way, *huwa* encompasses all the letters, which are the origins of the words, and flows through the whole of existence. Its dynamic, active quality again explains why the ontologically male pronoun 'He' is used to translate it.

Ibn 'Arabi says:

> There is nothing in existence except God, His names and His actions. He is the first with regard to His name apparent and the last with regard to His name hidden. So existence is all real.[20]

20. *Futuhat*, vol. III, p. 68; see also Chittick, *Sufi Path*, p. 133.

History of the translations

An English translation of this work was first published in the *Journal of the Royal Asiatic Society*, London, in 1901,[1] under the heading *Translation of an Arabic Manuscript in the Hunterian Collection, Glasgow University*. The translation begins with the copyist's attribution of the work to Ibn 'Arabi. The translator, T.H. Weir, also mentions four other manuscripts which he used in the translation all of which were attributed to Balyani or Balbani, apart from one Berlin manuscript attributed to Suyuti.

The Royal Asiatic Society continued to promote the work of Ibn 'Arabi by publishing an English translation of his famous book of mystical love poems *The Tarjuman al-Ashwaq* (*Interpreter of Ardent Desires*) in 1911 (since reprinted in 1978 by the Theosophical Society). There is no doubt that the *Tarjuman*, inspired by the beautiful Nizam whom he met in Mecca, was written by Ibn 'Arabi.

1. *Journal of the Royal Asiatic Society* (Oct. 1901), pp. 809–75.

Meanwhile, Abdul Hadi – otherwise known as the Swedish painter and author Ivan Aguéli, who initiated the well-known French scholar René Guénon into Sufism and founded the secret Sufi society Al-Akbariyya[2] in Paris in 1911 – published an Italian version of the treatise in 1907,[3] followed by a French translation which appeared in the journal *La Gnose* in Cairo in 1911. In the introduction to the French version, Abdul Hadi wrote that he was three-quarters of the way through his translation when he heard that the work had already been translated into English: 'I don't know where, or when, or by whom'. Although he notes that many manuscripts were attributed to Balyani or Balabani and other variations on the name,[4] as well as to Suyuti, he was inwardly convinced that its author was Ibn 'Arabi.

More recently, a study and translation published in 1982 by the French scholar and expert on Ibn

2. From the title the Shaykh al-Akbar (the Greatest Master) given to Ibn 'Arabi. The term 'akbarian' also comes from this title.

3. In *Il Convito–Al-Nadi* (Cairo, 1907).

4. Renditions into English depend on where the dots are placed on the Arabic letters.

'Arabi, Michel Chodkiewicz,[5] attempts to correct what he considers is a misattribution of the work to Ibn 'Arabi. He believes that it is the work of Awhad al-din Balyani (d.1287), also known as Abu 'Abdallah Balyani. James Winston Morris has confirmed Chodkiewicz's findings,[6] yet the attribution to Ibn 'Arabi, whether in actual fact or by inspiration, persists both in popular thought and even among scholars in some parts of the world. The name of Ibn 'Arabi therefore still appears on the cover of this edition, alongside that of Balyani. In this way, the alternative authorship is introduced and the continuing mention of Ibn 'Arabi's name helps to identify the work for those who are already familiar with it, since the title has many variations. Manuscripts attributed to both authors have been consulted in preparing the translation.

5. Michel Chodkiewicz, *Épître sur l'Unicité Absolue* (*Treatise on Absolute Unity – Risalat al-wahda al-mutlaqa*), (Paris: Les Deux Océans, 1982); see p. 19, n. 8.

6. James Winston Morris, 'Ibn 'Arabi and His Interpreters, Part II-A', in *Journal of the American Oriental Society*, vol. 106 (1986), pp. 733–56.

Manuscripts consulted

The translation was prepared consulting various manuscripts from the United Kingdom, Turkey and Syria. Of the five manuscripts used by T.H. Weir in his English translation, three have been consulted. The principal one is in the Hunterian collection (No. 456) in the University of Glasgow Library and is undated. However, according to an *ex libris* note, this was formerly in the collection of the French orientalist François Pétis de la Croix, who died in 1713 so it definitely predates this. It is attributed to Al-shaykh al-akbar Muhyi-al-din 'Arabi, and entitled *The Book of Answers* (*Kitab al-Ajwiba*) *also called The Book of Alif* (*Kitab al-Alif*): *On the explanation of the saying of the Prophet, peace on him, 'Whoever knows their self, knows their Lord'* (*man 'arafa nafsahu faqad 'arafa rabbahu*). Weir mentions that two of the other manuscripts he used were held in the British Museum, although they are now in the British Library (Add. 16839 and Or. 3684). They are both attributed to Balyani, who is described in one as 'The Pole of Poles (*qutb al-aqtab*)' Shaykh 'Abdallah al-Balyani and in the other he is called Auhad al

Din 'Abd-allah al-Balyani. The second of these is entitled *On the oneness of being and the knower of God* (*fi wahdat al-wujud wa fi-l-'arif*).

From Damascus, the two principal copies of manuscripts used by Michel Chodkiewicz in his French translation have been consulted. These were formerly in the Zahiriyya Library, and referred to by him as Z^1 and Z^2, but are now held in the Assad Library (mss. 6897 and 7965). The first is a late copy, being dated 1813, and is attributed to Shaykh 'Abd al-Balbani while the second is estimated by M. Chodkiewicz to be from the 16th or 17th century and is attributed to Shaykh 'Abd Allah al-Balyani.

From Turkey, four manuscripts have been used, two from the Suleymaniye Library in Istanbul (Shehit Ali 1344 and Yazma Bagislar 5935), one from the Inebey Library in Bursa (Genel 4420) and one from The National Library of Turkey in Ankara (Genel 4420). Two are attributed to Ibn 'Arabi and two to Balyani. The principal one from the Suleymaniye is relatively early, dateable from other works in the codex to 1542. The others are from the 17th, 18th and 19th centuries. Three of the copies are entitled *The Treatise on Unity* (*Risalat al-ahadiyya*).

Quotations from the Quran, hadith and other sayings

(in order of appearance in the text)

Whoever knows their self, knows their Lord.
(Hadith, saying attributed to the Prophet Muhammad)

And He is now as He has always been. *(Hadith)*

I knew my Lord through my Lord. *(Hadith)*

God is, and nothing is with Him. *(Hadith)*

O God, show me things as they are. *(Hadith)*

Everything passes away except His face. *(Q.28:88)*

I am the truth. *(An ecstatic saying of Hallaj)*

Glory to me. *(An ecstatic saying of Abu Yazid al-Bistami)*

Do not curse time, because God is time. *(Hadith)*

The high God says: 'O child of Adam, I was sick and you did not visit Me, I was hungry and you did not feed Me, I asked of you and you did not give to Me…'. *(Divine saying, hadith qudsi)*

Every day in a different configuration.

(Q.55:29)

He is the first and the last, the apparent and the hidden and He has knowledge of everything.

(Q.57:3)

Die before you die. (Hadith)

God says, 'My servant continues to approach Me with free acts until I love him. And when I love him, I am his hearing, his sight, his hand…'.

(Divine saying)

There is no god but God (*La ilaha illa llah*).
(*Muslim declaration of faith in God's unity, referred to as the Shahada*)

The faithful one is the mirror of the Faithful One.

(Hadith)

Eyes do not perceive Him but He perceives the eyes, He is the subtle and well-informed one.

(Q.6:103)

Bibliography

Abdul-Hadi (Ivan Aguéli), *L'Identité Suprême dans l'Ésotérisme Musulman: Le Traité de l'Unité* (*Risalatul-Ahadiyyah*) attributed to Mohyiddin Ibn 'Arabi, in *Le Voile d'Isis*, Paris, Jan. and Feb. 1933.

—— Reprinted from *La Gnose*, Paris, June, July and Aug. 1911.

—— First published by Abdul-Hadi in an Italian translation in the Arabic/Italian Journal *Il Convito–Al-Nadi*, Cairo, 1907.

—— Also published as: Al-Balabani, attributed to Ibn 'Arabi, *El Tratado de la Unidad*, Introduction and translation into French by Abdul-Hadi, and into Spanish by Victoria Argimón, ed. José J. De Olañeta, Barcelona: Los Pequeños Libros de la Sabiduría, 2004.

Austin, R.W.J. *Sufis of Andalusia*. Sherborne, Glos.: Beshara Publications, 1988.

Balyani, Awhad al-din. *Épître sur l'Unicité Absolue*. Introduction and translation by Michel Chodkiewicz. Paris: Les Deux Océans, 1982.

Burckhardt, Titus. *Mystical Astrology According to Ibn 'Arabi*. Aldsworth, Glos.: Beshara Publications, 1977.

Chittick, William C. *The Sufi Path of Knowledge*. Albany, NY: SUNY Press, 1989.

—— *The Self-Disclosure of God*. Albany, NY: SUNY Press, 1998.

Hirtenstein, Stephen. *The Unlimited Mercifier: The spiritual life and thought of Ibn 'Arabi*. Oxford: Anqa Publishing, 1999.

Ibn 'Arabi. 'A Treatise on The One Alone (*Kitab al-ahadiyyah*)'. In *Divine Governance of the Human Kingdom* (*At-Tadbirat al-ilahiyyah fi islah al-mamlakat al-insaniyyah*). Interpreted by Shaykh Tosun Bayrak al-Jerrahi al-Halveti. Louisville: Fons Vitae, 1997; pp. 231–53.

—— *Contemplation of the Holy Mysteries*. Translated by Cecilia Twinch and Pablo Beneito. Oxford: Anqa Publishing, 2001.

—— *Fusus al-hikam*. Ed. A. 'Affifi. Beirut: Dar al-Kitab al-'Arabi, 1946.

—— *The Bezels of Wisdom*. Translation and introduction by R.W.J. Austin. New York: Paulist Press, 1980.

—— *The Ringstones of Wisdom* (*Fusus al-hikam*). Translated by Caner K. Dagli. Chicago: Kazi Publications, 2004.

—— *The Wisdom of the Prophets* (Extracts from Ibn 'Arabi's *Fusus al-hikam*). Translated into the French by Titus Burckhardt and into the English by Angela Culme-Seymour. Aldsworth, Glos.: Beshara Publications, 1975.

—— *Ismail Hakki Bursevi's Translation of and Commentary on Fusus al-Hikam by Muhyiddin Ibn 'Arabi.* Rendered into English by Bulent Rauf with the help of R. Brass and H. Tollemache: 4 volumes. Vol. 1, Oxford and Istanbul 1986; Vols. 2, 3 & 4, Oxford, Istanbul and San Francisco 1987 & 1989: Muhyiddin Ibn 'Arabi Society.

—— *Al-Futuhat al-makkiyya.* Beirut: Dar Sadir, n.d.

—— *The Meccan Revelations.* Vol. I, 2002, Vol. II, 2004. Selected passages translated in M. Chodkiewicz (ed.) with W.C. Chittick, J.W. Morris, C. Chodkiewicz and D. Gril. [French to English translation by David Streight.] New York: Pir Press. See also Chittick, *Self-Disclosure* and *Sufi Path*, listed above, which also contain translations of selected passages.

—— *Kitab al-alif wa huwa Kitab al-ahadiyya.* In *Rasa'il Ibn 'Arabi*, Beirut: Dar Sadir, 1997, pp. 44–57. Translated into English by Abraham Abadi as *The Book of Alif (or) The Book of Unity*, in *Journal of the Muhyiddin Ibn 'Arabi Society*, 2, 1984, pp. 15–40.

—— *The Tarjuman al-Ashwaq: A Collection of Mystical Odes.* Translated by Reynold A. Nicholson. London: Theosophical Publishing House, 1978.

——*Stations of Desire: Love Elegies from Ibn 'Arabi and New Poems*. Includes modern translations of poems from the *Tarjuman al-Ashwaq* by Michael A. Sells. Jerusalem: Ibis Editions, 2000.

Jami, 'Abd al-Rahman. *Nafahat al-uns*. Tehran, 1957.

Lamborn Wilson, Peter. 'Quantum, Chaos, and the Oneness of Being: Meditations on the *Kitab al-Alef*'. In *Muhyiddin Ibn 'Arabi: A Commemorative Volume*. Edited by S. Hirtenstein and M. Tiernan. Shaftesbury, Dorset: Element, 1993.

Morris, James Winston. 'Ibn 'Arabi and His Interpreters, Part II-A'. In *Journal of the American Oriental Society*, vol. 106, 1986, pp. 733–56. See the Ibn 'Arabi Society website: http://www.ibnarabi-society.org/articles/interpreters.html pp. 6–15.

——'Jami's description of Abu Abdallah Balyani: Theophany or "Pantheism"?: the Importance of Balyani's *Risalat al-Ahadiyya*'. In *Horizons Maghrebins*, no. 30, Toulouse, Winter 1995, pp. 43–50.

——'Seeing Past the Shadows: Ibn 'Arabi's "Divine Comedy"'. In *Journal of the Muhyiddin Ibn 'Arabi Society*, 12, 1992, pp. 50–69.

Nasr, Seyyed Hossein. *Islamic Philosophy from its Origin to the Present*. Albany, NY: SUNY Press, 2006.

Qushayri, Abu'l-Qasim al-. *Al-Qushayri's Epistle on Sufism*. Translated by Alexander Knysh. Reading, UK: Garnet, 2007.

Weir, T.H. *Translation of an Arabic manuscript in the Hunterian Collection, Glasgow University.* Attributed principally to Ibnu'l 'Arabi, Art. XXIX, in *Journal of the Royal Asiatic Society.* London, Oct. 1901, pp. 809–25.

——Reprinted by Beshara Publications under the title: Ibn 'Arabi, *'Whoso Knoweth Himself…'* from the *Treatise on Being (Risale-t-ul-wujudiyyah),* London, 1976; and *'Whoso Knoweth Himself…': T.H. Weir's translation of the Treatise on Being attributed to Muhyiddin Ibn 'Arabi,* Northleach, Cheltenham, 2007.